# Flexible and Rigid

### Revised and Updated

Angela Royston

**www.heinemann.co.uk/library**
Visit our website to find out more information about Heinemann Library books.

To order:
☎ Phone 44 (0) 1865 888066
🖹 Send a fax to 44 (0) 1865 314091
💻 Visit the Heinemann Bookshop at www.heinemann.co.uk/library to browse our catalogue and order online.

First published in Great Britain by Heinemann Library, Halley Court, Jordan Hill, Oxford OX2 8EJ, part of Pearson Education. Heinemann is a registered trademark of Pearson Education Ltd.

Editorial: Diyan Leake
Design: Joanna Hinton-Malivoire
Picture research: Melissa Allison and Mica Brancic
Production: Alison Parsons

Originated by Chroma Graphics (Overseas) Pte Ltd
Printed and bound in China by South China Printing Co. Ltd

ISBN 978 0 431 13778 0 (hardback)
12 11 10 09 08
10 9 8 7 6 5 4 3 2 1

ISBN 978 0 431 13836 7 (paperback)
12 11 10 09 08
10 9 8 7 6 5 4 3 2 1

**British Library Cataloguing in Publication Data**
Royston, Angela
Flexible and rigid. - New ed. - (My world of science)
  1. Flexure - Juvenile literature
  I. Title II. Royston, Angela. Bendy and rigid
  620.1'1244

**Acknowledgements**
The publishers would like to thank the following for permission to reproduce photographs: © Alamy p. **16** (Forrest Smyth); © Chris Honeywell p. **26**; © David Bradford p. **24**; © Eye Ubiquitous pp. **9**, **29** (Chris Fairclough); © Getty Images pp. **20**, **25**; © Photodisc p. **17**; © Powerstock Zefa p. **12**; © Rupert Horrox p. **8**; © Trevor Clifford pp. **4**, **5**, **6**, **7**, **10**, **11**, **13**, **14**, **15**, **18**, **19**, **21**, **22**, **23**, **27**, **28**.

Cover photograph reproduced with permission of © Masterfile (Royalty Free).

The publishers would like to thank Jon Bliss for his assistance in the preparation of this book.

Every effort has been made to contact copyright holders of any material reproduced in this book. Any omissions will be rectified in subsequent printings if notice is given to the publishers.

# Contents

Any words appearing in the text in bold, **like this**, are explained in the glossary.

# What is flexible?

You can bend things that are flexible. This toy snake is flexible. You can bend it into different shapes. Which letter does it make here? (Answer on page 31.)

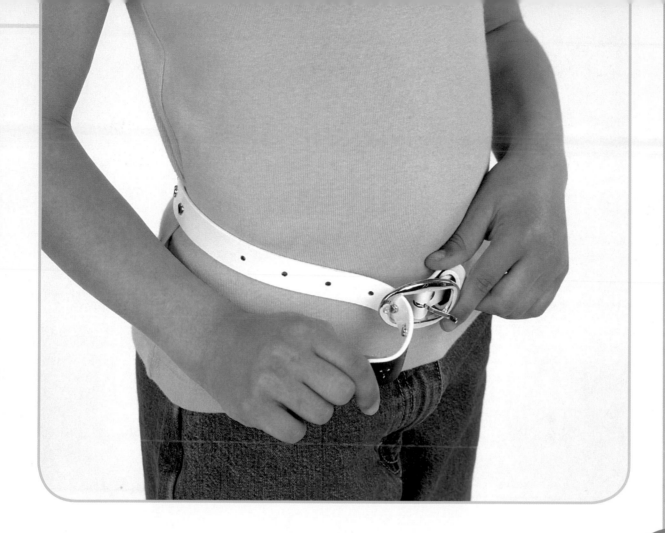

Some things have to be flexible to work properly. This girl is trying on a belt. She bends it round her waist and through the buckle.

# How flexible is it?

Playing cards can bend more than a ruler. Metal wire can be bent into paperclips. A rope needs to be very flexible to be useful.

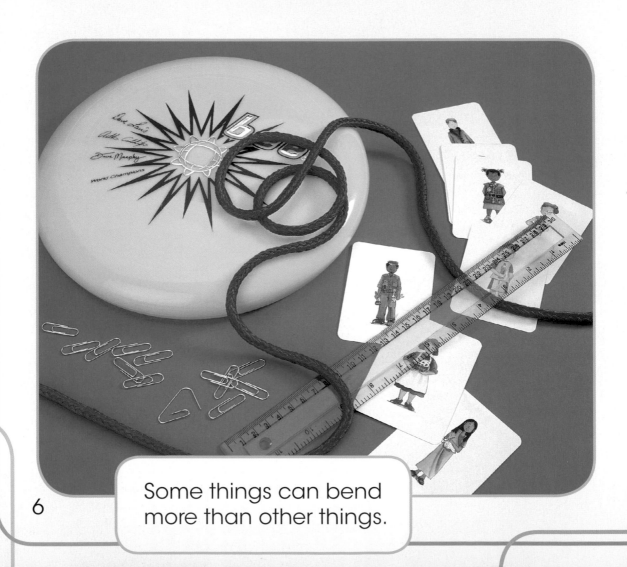

Some things can bend more than other things.

These children are testing shoes. They are seeing how much each shoe can bend without breaking. Which shoe is the most flexible? (Answer on page 31.)

# What is rigid?

If something is rigid, you cannot change its shape by bending it. No matter how much you push or pull it, it stays the same shape.

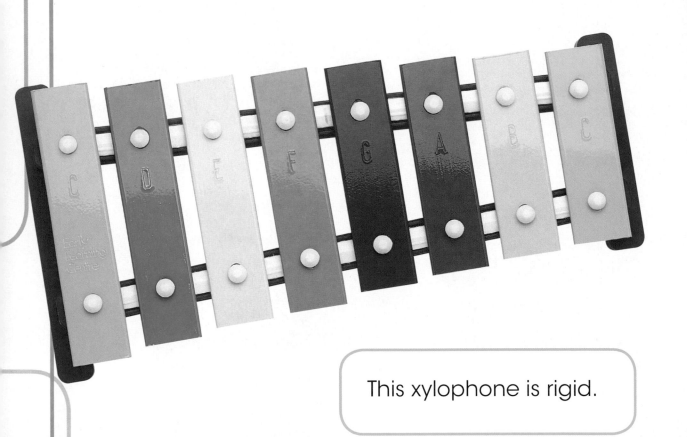

This xylophone is rigid.

This pan and plate are both rigid.

Some things need to be rigid to be useful. You can put things on something rigid. You can use rigid things to carry other things.

# How rigid is it?

Wood is quite rigid. It keeps its shape unless you bend it. Even then it only bends a little bit. A thick piece of wood might not bend at all.

A wooden ruler is quite rigid, but you can bend it a bit.

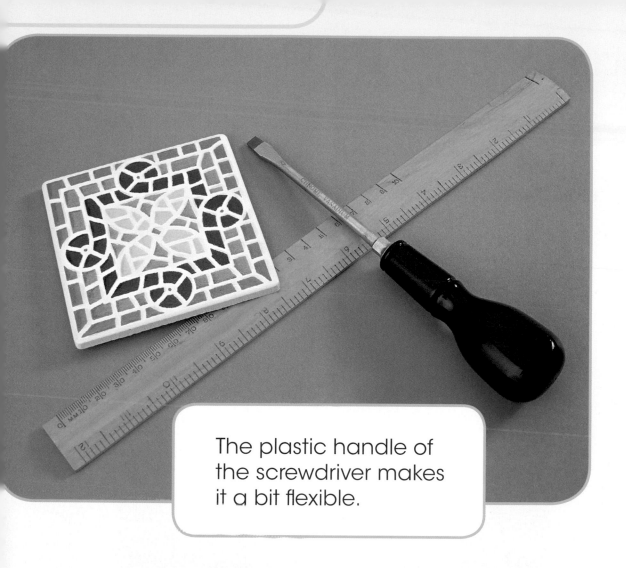

The plastic handle of the screwdriver makes it a bit flexible.

The **screwdriver** is more rigid than the wooden ruler. But the most rigid thing in the photo is the tile. The tile will not bend at all.

# Plastic

Some plastic is flexible. This coat is made of a kind of plastic. Being flexible makes it easier to put on and to move around in.

This plastic **hosepipe** is very flexible. It can be wound into a circle when it is not being used. But the plastic watering can is rigid.

# Wheels

Bicycle wheels have **rubber** tyres.
Rubber is strong but flexible. It bends as
you go over a bump in the path.

Bicycle wheels have a rigid **rim** and rigid **spokes**. The rim and the spokes hold the wheels in shape. What shape are the rims in this picture? (Answer on page 31.)

spokes

rim

# Shoes

Most shoes are flexible. This allows you to bend your foot. The bottom of a shoe is made of strong plastic or **leather**.

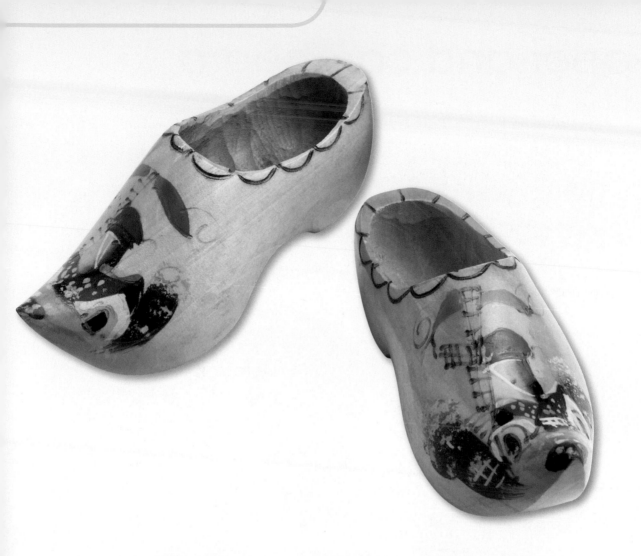

These **clogs** are made of wood. The wood is rigid and does not bend as you walk. It is not very easy to walk in clogs.

# Paper and cardboard

A sheet of paper is very flexible. It can be rolled into a tube or folded several times. When you unroll the sheet it becomes flat again.

Cardboard is thicker and more rigid than paper. It does not bend easily. Thick cardboard is used to make strong, rigid boxes.

# Thick and thin

It is easier to bend something that is thin than something that is thick. These thick **girders** will not bend easily. They make a rigid steel frame.

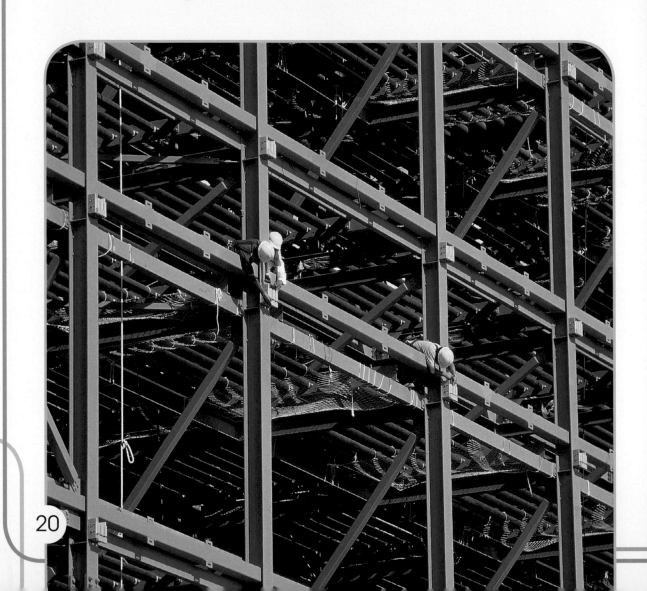

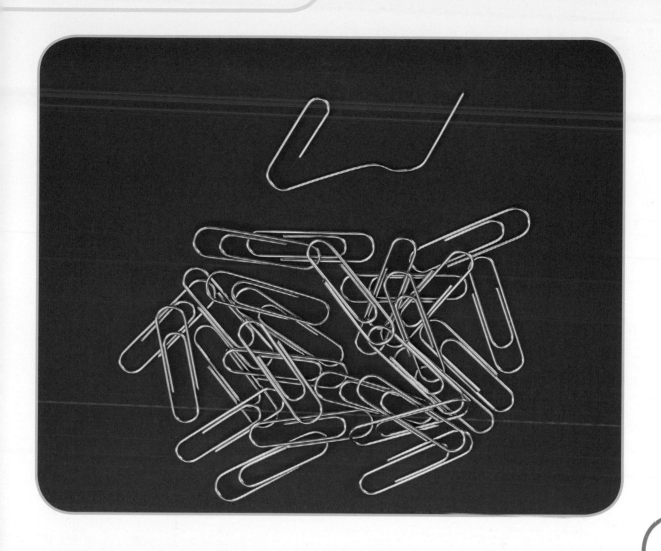

These paperclips are made of steel, just like the girders. But the paperclips are thin. This makes them easy to bend.

# Bending and breaking

Most flexible things can only bend a certain amount. Then they break. This stick has been bent so far that it has broken into two pieces.

This spoon has been bent by mistake.

If a spoon is bent backwards and forwards over and over again, the metal will become weaker. The spoon may snap in two.

# Wood can bend

Sometimes wood can bend. This cat's basket is made out of wooden twigs. The twigs are bent and twisted together.

Trees bend when they are blown by strong winds. The leaves of these palm trees are being bent by a **hurricane**. Bending stops the trees from being blown over.

# China is brittle

Rigid things do not bend, but they break. Some rigid things are **brittle**. This means that they crack or break easily.

These china cups and saucers are brittle.

Plates, mugs, bowls, and ornaments are often made of **china**. Be careful not to drop china! If it is dropped, it may break into many pieces.

# Other brittle materials

Glass is even more **brittle** than **china**, especially if it is thin. Very fine glass can be **fragile**. This means that it breaks easily.

These glasses are very fragile.

Stones and bricks are brittle, too. But they are so thick they do not break easily. This worker is using a **sledgehammer** to break up the stone.

# Glossary

**brittle**  easy to break into pieces

**china**  material that is often used to make plates, bowls, cups, and vases

**clog**  shoe with a bottom made of wood

**fragile**  easy to break or to damage

**girder**  thick piece of steel used to hold up a building

**hosepipe**  long tube that carries water from a tap

**hurricane**  storm that includes very strong wind and very heavy rain

**leather**  material made from the skin of a cow or other animal

**rim**  edge

**rubber**  flexible material made from the sap of the rubber tree

**screwdriver**  tool used to screw nails into wood

**sledgehammer**  big, heavy hammer

**spokes**  set of thin rods that join the rim of a wheel to its centre

# Answers

**Page 4 –** The snake makes the shape of the letter S.

**Page 7 –** The girl in the middle has the most flexible shoe.

**Page 15 –** Each wheel rim makes the shape of a circle.

# More books to read

*Materials: What Is Stuff Made Of?* (Ticktock Media, 2005)

*Materials: Wood*, Chris Oxlade (Heinemann Library, 2002)

*Using Materials: How We Use Plastic*, Chris Oxlade (Heinemann Library, 2004)

# Index